Bocas del Toro, Beach Adventures

D1737199

Eunice M. McCal

The Complete & current Guide to one of Panamá's most beautiful beaches with planning, transportation, accommodation, activities, attractions, safety tips, etc.

Table of Contents

Chapter 1

Bocas del Toro

1.1 Overview of Bocas del Toro.

Bocas del Toro, located in northern Panama, is a picturesque archipelago of islands, islets, and cays scattered over the Caribbean Sea. Bocas del Toro, known for its stunning beaches, thick forests, and vibrant culture, offers a one-of-a-kind tropical paradise for travelers seeking adventure, pleasure, and exploration.

Geographical Features:
Bocas del Toro is made up of many big islands, including Isla Colón, Isla Bastimentos, Isla Carenero, and Isla Solarte, each with its own unique beauty and attractions. The archipelago is known for its emerald-green oceans, thick mangrove forests, and spectacular coral reefs teeming with marine life.

Cultural Diversity:
One of the most appealing aspects of Bocas del Toro is its diverse cultural heritage, which

combines indigenous communities, Afro-Caribbean influences, and European immigration. The region is home to various ethnic groups, including the Ngäbe-Buglé, Guna, and Afro-Panamanian people, all of whom contribute to the intricate fabric of Bocas del Toro's cultural identity.

Ecological Importance:
Bocas del Toro is regarded as a biodiversity hotspot, with a diverse range of unusual plant and animal species found nowhere else on Earth. The archipelago is part of the Mesoamerican Barrier Reef System, the world's second-largest coral reef system, making it an ideal destination for snorkelers, divers, and marine enthusiasts.

Tourism Hub:
Bocas del Toro has recently emerged as a popular destination for eco-tourism, adventure seekers, and those looking to escape the hustle and bustle of city life. Bocas del Toro offers a wide range of activities for all types of tourists,

from relaxing beach resorts to adrenaline-pumping water sports.

Sustainable Development:
With its growing popularity, Bocas del Toro has the challenge of balancing visitor expansion with environmental conservation. Sustainable tourism initiatives and community-based projects are now underway to preserve the region's natural beauty and cultural legacy for future generations to enjoy.

In essence, Bocas del Toro is more than just a tourist destination; it is a haven where nature, culture, and adventure come together to create unforgettable experiences. Whether you want to find solitude on quiet beaches, explore beautiful underwater habitats, or immerse yourself in the rich tapestry of Caribbean culture, Bocas del Toro welcomes you with open arms to embark on a journey of discovery and adventure.

1.2 History & Culture

Historical Background: Bocas del Toro's history is a rich tapestry of indigenous peoples, European explorers, and Afro-Caribbean residents. The region's original inhabitants were indigenous tribes such as the Ngäbe-Buglé and the Guna, who coexisted peacefully with nature and relied on fishing and agriculture for survival.

In the early 16th century, Spanish explorers were drawn to the region by reports of gold and other minerals. However, it was not until the nineteenth century that Bocas del Toro began to attract significant attention due to its strategic location along trade routes and abundant natural resources.

During the late nineteenth and early twentieth centuries, Bocas del Toro experienced an influx of Caribbean immigrants, primarily from Jamaica, who came to work in the region's expanding banana industry. Their cultural influence can still be seen today in the archipelago's large Afro-Caribbean communities.

Cultural Diversity: Bocas del Toro's cultural environment combines indigenous traditions, Afro-Caribbean rhythms, and Hispanic influences. Visitors can immerse themselves in the rich tapestry of local culture by experiencing traditional music, dance, food, and artisan crafts.

Throughout the year, the area celebrates a variety of cultural festivals and events, including the colorful Carnaval festivities, which feature lively parades, music, and dance performances.

1.3 Climate and Ideal Time to Visit

Climate Overview:

Bocas del Toro has a tropical marine environment characterized by moderate temperatures, high humidity, and heavy rainfall all year. The area has two distinct seasons: dry and rainy.

- Dry Season (December to April): The dry season is regarded as the best time to visit Bocas del Toro, with bright days, clear skies, and low rainfall. Visitors may anticipate pleasant temperatures ranging from 25°C to 32°C (77°F to 90°F), making it perfect for outdoor sports and beach visits.

- Rainy Season (May to November): The rainy season brings higher precipitation and sometimes thunderstorms to Bocas del Toro. While rainfall may be substantial at times, it typically happens in brief, powerful spurts, followed by spells of sunlight. Despite the rain, the lush jungles come alive this season, delivering stunning landscapes and vivid animal interactions.

Best Time to Visit:
The ideal time to visit Bocas del Toro depends on your choices and interests. For tourists seeking sunny weather and outdoor experiences, the dry season (December to April) is the best time to enjoy the region's beautiful beaches, coral reefs, and hiking trails.

However, if you're interested in enjoying the lush grandeur of Bocas del Toro's rainforests and taking advantage of reduced lodging costs, the rainy season (May to November) gives you a unique chance to immerse yourself in the region's natural majesty while avoiding the crowds.

Ultimately, regardless of the season, Bocas del Toro welcomes travelers year-round with its warm hospitality, stunning scenery, and strong cultural legacy, providing a memorable tropical escape for adventurers and explorers alike.

Chapter 2

Plan Your Trip

2.1 Setting Your Travel Budget

Planning your vacation to Bocas del Toro starts with establishing a reasonable travel budget to guarantee a memorable and pleasurable experience without breaking the bank. Here are some crucial measures to help you set your vacation budget effectively:

1. Determine Your Total Available Funds:
Begin by examining your entire financial status and estimating how much you can afford to spend on your vacation to Bocas del Toro. Consider aspects such as your salary, savings, and any other sources of financing available for trip expenditures.

2. Break Down Your Expenses:
Identify and classify the different expenditures related to your vacation, including transportation, housing, food, activities, mementos, and other fees. Breaking down your

spending into particular categories can help you acquire a greater picture of where your money will be spent.

3. Research Destination Costs:
Research the typical expenses of products and services in Bocas del Toro, including lodging rates, restaurant pricing, transportation fees, and activity expenditures. Websites, travel guides, and internet forums may give helpful insights into the normal expenditures involved with traveling to and within the area.

4. Set Priorities and Allocate Funds Accordingly:
Prioritize your travel choices and spend finances appropriately to guarantee that you can afford the activities that matter most to you. Determine which components of your vacation are non-negotiables and be prepared to change your budget appropriately to meet them.

5. Consider Seasonal Variations:
Take into consideration seasonal differences in travel prices and availability while arranging your vacation to Bocas del Toro. Peak tourist seasons may correspond with higher prices for lodging and activities, while off-season vacation provides the chance for reduced rates and fewer people.

6. Factor in Contingency Funds:
Allocate a percentage of your travel budget for unforeseen costs and emergencies that may happen during your trip. Having a contingency fund accessible can give you peace of mind and guarantee that you're prepared to manage any unanticipated problems without sacrificing your vacation pleasure.

7. Monitor and Adjust Your Budget as Needed:
Continuously analyze your expenditures and change your budget as required to remain within your financial boundaries. Be wary of overpaying in specific areas and seek chances to save money without jeopardizing the quality of your trip.

By establishing a reasonable trip budget and preparing ahead, you may optimize your pleasure of Bocas del Toro while keeping within your financial limits. Remember to prioritize activities that correspond with your interests and tastes, and don't hesitate to seek out cost-effective alternatives to make the most of your vacation.

2.2 Choosing the Right Accommodation

Selecting the correct lodging is vital to ensuring a pleasant and pleasurable stay during your vacation to Bocas del Toro. Here are some crucial aspects to help you find the best hotel option:

1. Location:
Consider the location of your hotel in relation to the sites and activities you wish to discover in Bocas del Toro. Whether you choose a beachfront resort, a comfortable guesthouse in town, or a remote eco-lodge in the jungle, select a place that corresponds with your travel plan and tastes.

2. Amenities & Facilities:

Evaluate the services and facilities given by possible hotel alternatives, such as Wi-Fi access, air conditioning, hot water, free breakfast, swimming pools, and on-site food options. Determine which facilities are vital for your comfort and convenience throughout your visit.

3. Budget:

Establish a budget for lodging expenditures based on your entire trip budget and financial goals. Bocas del Toro provides a choice of housing alternatives to suit any budget, from budget-friendly hostels and guesthouses to luxury resorts and eco-lodges. Compare pricing and facilities to discover the greatest value for your money.

4. Reviews and Recommendations:

Research online reviews and suggestions from prior guests to acquire insights into the quality and reputation of possible lodging alternatives. Websites like TripAdvisor, Booking.com, and

Airbnb include user-generated reviews and ratings to help you make educated selections.

5. Safety and security:
Prioritize safety and security while picking hotel alternatives in Bocas del Toro. Choose reputed businesses with sufficient security measures in place, such as safe locks, 24-hour front desk service, and well-lit premises, to guarantee a worry-free stay.

6. Sustainability and Eco-Friendliness:
Consider staying at eco-friendly and sustainable lodging alternatives that stress environmental protection and ethical tourist practices. Many hotels and resorts in Bocas del Toro are devoted to eco-friendly programs, such as energy saving, trash reduction, and community participation.

2.3 Packing Essentials for Your Trip

Packing intelligently ensures that you have all you need for a comfortable and pleasurable vacation to Bocas del Toro. Here's a list of necessary goods to consider bringing for your adventure:

1. Lightweight Clothing:
Pack lightweight, breathable clothes ideal for the tropical environment of Bocas del Toro. Include clothes such as T-shirts, shorts, swimsuits, sundresses, and comfortable walking shoes for touring the islands and beaches.

2. Sun Protection:
Bring sun protection necessities, like sunscreen with a high SPF, sunglasses, wide-brimmed hats, and lightweight clothes with UPF protection to shield your skin from the sun's rays during outdoor activities.

3. Insect Repellent:
Protect yourself against mosquitoes and other insects by bringing insect repellent containing DEET or picaridin. Consider carrying long-sleeved shirts and slacks for further protection, particularly at dawn and twilight when mosquitoes are most active.

4. Waterproof Gear:
Prepare for the occasional rain showers in Bocas del Toro by carrying waterproof clothing such as a lightweight rain jacket, waterproof backpack or dry bag, and waterproof phone case to keep your possessions dry while exploring.

5. Travel Essentials:
Don't forget to pack important trip materials such as travel papers (passport, visa, travel insurance), electronic gadgets and chargers, reusable water bottles, a first-aid kit, and any required medicines or prescriptions.

6. Eco-Friendly Products:
Consider carrying eco-friendly and sustainable items, such as reusable water bottles, eco-friendly toiletries (shampoo, conditioner, soap), and biodegradable sunscreen and insect repellant to reduce your environmental effects throughout your vacation.

7. Adventure Gear:

If you want to indulge in outdoor activities such as snorkeling, diving, hiking, or surfing, remember to take the necessary gear and equipment, including snorkel mask and fins, diving certification card, hiking shoes, and surfboard (if applicable).

By packing intelligently and considering your unique travel requirements and tastes, you can ensure a hassle-free and pleasurable trip enjoying the natural beauty and cultural diversity of Bocas del Toro.

Chapter 3

Getting to Bocas del Toro

3.1 Air Travel Options

Bocas del Toro is accessible mostly by air, allowing passengers simple and fast air travel alternatives to reach this interesting region. Here are the primary plane travel alternatives available for reaching Bocas del Toro:

1. Flights to Bocas del Toro International Airport (BOC):
Bocas del Toro International Airport (BOC) serves as the principal entrance to the archipelago and is situated on Isla Colón, the main island of Bocas del Toro. Several airlines serve domestic flights from Panama City's Tocumen International Airport (PTY) to Bocas del Toro International Airport (BOC), providing varied daily flights to meet travelers' schedules.

2. Airlines Serving Bocas del Toro:
other airlines serve flights to Bocas del Toro International Airport (BOC), including Air Panama, Copa Airlines, and other smaller carriers. Flight lengths from Panama City to Bocas del Toro normally run from 45 minutes to 1 hour, offering passengers a practical and time-efficient way of visiting the archipelago.

3. Flight Availability and Booking:
Flights to Bocas del Toro are accessible throughout the week, with several departures and arrivals each day. It is advisable to book your flights in advance, particularly during high travel seasons, to secure preferred travel dates and take advantage of any available discounts or specials.

4. Connecting Flights & Travel Routes:
In addition to direct flights from Panama City to Bocas del Toro, guests may also have the option to book connecting flights via smaller airports such as David or Changuinola, depending on the airline and travel schedule. Connecting flights gives flexibility in travel

plans and may provide a chance to explore other regions of Panama before reaching Bocas del Toro.

5. Arrival and Ground Transportation:
Upon arriving at Bocas del Toro International Airport (BOC), guests may conveniently receive ground transportation alternatives to reach their accommodations or specified sites around the archipelago. Taxi services, shuttle buses, and water taxis are easily available at the airport terminal to bring tourists to various regions of Isla Colón and adjacent islands.

6. Travel Tips:
- Verify airline Schedules: Be cautious to verify airline schedules and availability in advance, especially during major travel seasons and holidays.
- Arrive Early: Arrive at the airport well in advance of your intended departure time to allow for check-in, security screening, and boarding procedures.

- Pack Light: Consider packing light to save additional baggage charges and allow easier transportation to and from the airport.
- Confirm Ground Transportation: Confirm ground transportation arrangements from the airport to your hotel in advance to ensure a flawless and hassle-free arrival experience.

By picking air travel possibilities to Bocas del Toro, guests may have easy access to this tropical paradise and begin an exciting journey of exploration and discovery amid the outstanding natural beauty of Panama's Caribbean coast.

3.2 Land and Sea Transportation

While air travel is the most regular way to reach Bocas del Toro, land and maritime transportation choices are also accessible for individuals seeking different routes or visiting adjacent locations of Panama. Here are the key land and sea transportation choices to consider:

1. Shuttle Buses and Taxis:
Shuttle buses and taxis provide quick transportation possibilities for tourists coming from smaller airports such as David or Changuinola, which are located on the mainland near Bocas del Toro. Shuttle services and taxis may bring tourists from these airports to Almirante, a seaside town on the mainland, where water taxis are available for passage to Bocas del Toro.

2. Water Taxis and Boats:
Water taxis and boats are the predominant types of transportation for going between mainland Panama and the islands of Bocas del Toro. Water taxis operate regular services between Almirante and several places around the archipelago, including Isla Colón, Isla Bastimentos, and other adjacent islands. Travelers may easily acquire water taxi services from the mainland port at Almirante to reach their desired island location in Bocas del Toro.

3. Private Boat Charters:

For clients wishing a more tailored and flexible transportation option, private boat trips are provided for rent in Bocas del Toro. Private boat charters offer individualized itineraries and may transport tourists to far beaches, peaceful islands, and hidden coves around the archipelago, giving a unique and memorable holiday experience.

4. Rental Cars and Scooters:

While rental automobiles and scooters are not commonly employed for traveling within the islands of Bocas del Toro due to limited road infrastructure and the prevalence of water transportation, they may be great for seeing the mainland regions of Panama before or after visiting the archipelago. Rental car corporations operate in key cities and airports across Panama, enabling a convenient form of transportation for visitors visiting the country by land.

3.3 Entry Requirements and Visa Information

Before preparing for your holiday to Bocas del Toro, it is necessary to educate yourself on the admission requirements and visa information for visiting Panama. Here's what you should know:

1. Passport Requirements:

All travelers visiting Panama must have a passport that is valid for at least six months beyond their stated departure date. To avoid any entry issues when you arrive in Panama, make sure your passport is in perfect condition and free of damage or modifications.

2. Visa Requirements:

Citizens of various countries, including the United States, Canada, the European Union, Australia, and many Latin American countries, do not need a visa to visit Panama for tourism purposes. Travelers from visa-exempt countries are often awarded a tourist visa upon arrival in Panama, allowing for stays of up to 180 days.

3. Visa extensions:

If you want to remain in Panama for more than the initial 180 days, you may apply for a visa extension via the National Immigration Service (Servicio Nacional de Migración) in Panama City or regional immigration offices around the country. Visa extensions are subject to approval and may require payment of additional fees.

4. Return Ticket Requirements:

Panamanian immigration officers may require visitors to provide proof of onward travel, such as a return or onward plane ticket, indicating their intention to leave the country within the authorized length of stay. To satisfy this requirement, be prepared to provide your return ticket or travel itinerary when you arrive in Panama.

5. Yellow Fever Vaccine:

Travelers arriving from countries with a risk of yellow fever transmission may be required to provide a valid yellow fever vaccination certificate upon entrance to Panama. Check Panama's current health and immunization standards before coming to ensure compliance with any mandatory vaccination laws.

By studying the entry requirements and visa information for Panama, you can ensure a smooth and hassle-free arrival process and focus on enjoying your trip in the breathtaking landscapes and rich culture of Bocas del Toro.

Chapter 4

Exploring Bocas Town.

4.1 Overview of Bocas Town.

Bocas Town, the main hub of the Bocas del Toro archipelago, is a charming and vibrant beach town located on Isla Colón. Bocas Town, the area's commercial and cultural hub, offers a one-of-a-kind blend of Caribbean charm, a relaxed atmosphere, and bustling activity. Here's an overview of what you may expect when seeing Bocas Town:

1. Colorful Architecture:
Bocas Town is known for its colorful wooden residences, vibrant facades, and stunning seaside promenades. Stroll around the streets of Bocas Town and see the diverse architecture that reflects the town's rich history and cultural culture.

2. Bustling Waterfront:
The waterfront area of Bocas Town is bustling with activity, with boats arriving and departing,

fishermen unloading their catch of the day, and waterfront restaurants and bars offering breathtaking views of the Caribbean Sea. Take a leisurely walk along the waterfront promenade and absorb the lively atmosphere of this coastal town.

3. Local Markets and Shops:
Bocas Town is home to a number of local markets, shops, and boutiques where you may purchase souvenirs, handicrafts, and locally manufactured things. Explore the bustling markets and purchase handmade jewelry, artisanal crafts, vivid textiles, and other one-of-a-kind items created by local artisans.

4. Dining and Culinary delights:
Bocas Town has a vibrant culinary scene, with several restaurants, cafés, and diners serving a wide range of cuisines to suit any taste. From fresh seafood and Caribbean delicacies to international fare and fusion cuisine, Bocas Town offers a diverse dining experience that celebrates the region's gastronomical richness.

5. Vibrant nightlife:
As the sun sets over the Caribbean Sea, Bocas Town comes alive with a thriving nightlife and entertainment scene. Explore the lively pubs, beach bars, and waterfront discos where you can dance the night away to the rhythms of reggae, salsa, and calypso music.

6. Water Activities and Excursions:
Bocas Town serves as the starting point for a variety of water activities and excursions, including snorkeling, diving, surfing, and island hopping. Take a boat tour of the adjacent islands, discover hidden coves and beautiful beaches, or dive into the crystal-clear waters to witness colorful coral reefs and aquatic life.

7. Cultural immersion:
Visit local festivals, cultural events, and community celebrations to learn about Bocas Town's vibrant culture and traditions. Bocas Town offers opportunities to engage with locals and enjoy the rich tapestry of Caribbean culture, including traditional dances and music

performances, as well as art exhibitions and cultural lectures.

Bocas Town is a captivating destination that captures the essence of Caribbean charm, natural beauty, and cultural vibrancy. Whether you're meandering along the beach, eating local food, or diving into the Caribbean's azure waters, Bocas Town invites you to embark on an unforgettable journey of adventure and discovery in the heart of the Bocas del Toro archipelago.

4.2 Popular Restaurants and Cafés

Bocas Town has a diverse gastronomic culture, with restaurants and cafés catering to every taste and price. Here are some popular food establishments to find when visiting Bocas Town:

1. Buenavista Restaurant & Bar:
Buena Vista Restaurant & Bar, located on the waterfront promenade, offers beautiful views of the Caribbean Sea while serving up superb seafood dishes, Caribbean favorites, and

refreshing cocktails in a relaxed and cheerful atmosphere.

2. The Ultimate Refuge:

El Ultimo Refugio, known for its diverse menu and imaginative fusion cuisine, is a favorite among both locals and visitors. Enjoy amazing seafood ceviche, gourmet pizzas, and one-of-a-kind cocktails in a lively setting, accompanied by live music and entertainment.

3. Bibi's at the Beach:

Bibi's on the Beach, located on Isla Carenero and just a short water taxi ride from Bocas Town, offers seaside eating with a relaxed atmosphere. Enjoy scrumptious seafood platters, grilled specialties, and tropical cocktails while taking in the sun-drenched views of the Caribbean.

4. Om Café and Bakery:

Begin your day with a delicious breakfast or brunch at Om Cafe & Bakery, a quaint café known for its organic coffee, artisan pastries, and nutritious menu options. Relax in the tranquil garden setting and enjoy the aromas of freshly made coffee and delectable baked goods.

5. Toro Loco Steakhouse:
Are you craving a beefy steak or grilled meat dish? Toro Loco Steakhouse offers a unique eating experience. Choose from a variety of prime steaks, grilled seafood, and delectable sides, all accompanied by excellent wines and drinks and served in a friendly and classy setting.

4.3 Nightlife and Entertainment Options.

When the sun goes down, Bocas Town comes alive with thriving nightlife and entertainment options that cater to all interests and preferences. Here are some of the best nightlife spots to visit in Bocas Town:

1. Aqua Lounge:
Aqua Lounge is a popular waterfront bar and nightclub situated on a floating pier in the heart of Bocas Town. Dance the night away under the stars in a colorful atmosphere with

tropical cocktails and live DJs playing the latest beats.

2. Barco Hundido:
Barco Hundido, a floating bar and restaurant built on top of a submerged shipwreck in Bocas Bay, offers a one-of-a-kind nightlife experience. Sip on inventive cocktails, sample fresh ceviche, and soak up the stunning views of the Caribbean while enjoying live music and entertainment.

3. Mondo Taitu:
Mondo Taitu is a popular backpacker hangout and live music venue known for its relaxed atmosphere and diverse events. Join other travelers for open mic nights, live band performances, and themed parties while enjoying cool drinks and refreshments.

4. Selina Bocas de Toro:
Selina Bocas del Toro is a contemporary hostel and entertainment complex that hosts a variety of events, such as dance nights, movie screenings, and beach parties. Relax in the

hostel's nice common areas, meet other visitors, and enjoy the lively social environment.

5. La Iguana Surf Club:

If you like surfing, don't miss La Iguana Surf Club, a seaside surf club and hangout where you can catch great waves during the day and enjoy live music and drinks at night. Join surfers from all over the world for cool cocktails, delicious seafood, and breathtaking sunsets.

Whether you're looking for great cuisine, live music, or unique nightlife experiences, Bocas Town has a wide range of options to fit every taste and mood. From riverside restaurants to seaside bars, Bocas Town invites you to immerse yourself in the vibrant culture and excitement of Panama's Caribbean coast.

Chapter 5

Island Hopping Itineraries

5.1 Day Trips to Nearby Islands.

Island hopping is a must-do activity while visiting Bocas del Toro since it allows visitors to enjoy the archipelago's diverse landscapes, stunning beaches, and colorful marine life. Here are some wonderful day excursions to nearby islands that you won't want to miss:

1. Isla Bastimentos:
- Begin your day with a boat tour to Isla Bastimentos, the archipelago's largest island, known for its lush woods, lonely beaches, and diverse wildlife.
- Explore Bastimentos National Aquatic Park, which is home to mangrove forests, coral reefs, and stunning snorkeling spots teeming with colorful fish and aquatic animals.
- Visit Red Frog Beach, one of Bocas del Toro's most well-known beaches, named for the region's little red poison dart frogs. Relax on the wonderful white sand beach, swim in the

crystal-clear waters, and walk along the woodland walkways that surround the beach.

- Explore the laid-back town of Old Bank, where you can interact with locals, eat traditional cuisine, and feel the true essence of Caribbean island life.

2. Isla Carnero:

- Take a short boat ride to Isla Carenero, a small island located only a stone's throw from Bocas Town and known for its tranquil beaches, vibrant coral reefs, and excellent snorkeling opportunities.

- Spend the day exploring the coral gardens and underwater ecosystems of Carenero's coastline, where you may encounter a wide range of tropical fish, sea turtles, and other marine animals.

- Take a leisurely beach picnic or dine at one of the island's waterfront restaurants, where you can savor wonderful seafood and tropical cocktails while admiring the breathtaking views of the Caribbean.

- Explore the island's lush interior on foot or by bicycle, following spectacular routes that wind through deep mangrove forests, secluded coves, and remote beaches.

3. Isla Zapatilla:
- Take a full-day boat cruise to Isla Zapatilla, a picturesque and uninhabited island located inside the Bastimentos National Marine Park.
- Spend the day snorkeling in the crystal-clear waters around the island, where you can see vibrant coral reefs, rare fish species, and other marine life.
- Unwind on Isla Zapatilla's immaculate white sand beaches, basking in the sun, swimming in the turquoise waters, and savoring the tranquility of this remote tropical paradise.
- Join a guided nature trip through the island's gorgeous rainforest to see indigenous species such as sloths, monkeys, and tropical birds, as well as learn about the island's unique ecosystem and conservation efforts.

These day trip itineraries are simply a sampling of the various choices for island exploration and adventure in Bocas del Toro. Whether you're diving amid coral reefs, resting on remote beaches, or hiking through forest pathways, island hopping in Bocas del Toro offers unforgettable experiences and breathtaking natural beauty at every turn.

5.2 Activities and Attractions for Each Island

Exploring the islands of Bocas del Toro offers a wide range of activities and attractions to suit any traveler's interests. Here's a taste of the activities and attractions you may enjoy on each island.

1. Isla Colon:
- Bocas Town: Discover the vibrant streets, beachfront promenades, and lively markets of Bocas Town.
- Surfing: Catch large waves at popular surfing spots such as Playa Bluff and Paunch Beach.
- Nature trips: Explore the island's stunning rainforests, mangrove swamps, and hidden waterfalls.
- Dolphin Watching: Take a dolphin-watching expedition to see pods of lively dolphins playing in the surrounding waters.

2. Isla Bastimentos:

- Red Frog Beach: Relax on the wonderful white sand beach, swim in the crystal-clear waters, and explore the forest pathways.
- Snorkeling and Diving: Bastimentos National Marine Park offers brilliant coral reefs, underwater tunnels, and unusual marine species.
- Kayaking and paddleboarding: Use a kayak or paddleboard to explore the serene mangrove woodlands and secluded coves.
- Jungle Trekking: Join a guided jungle trek through Bastimentos' rainforest pathways, which are home to sloths, monkeys, and unique birds.

3. Isla Carnero:

- Snorkeling and Diving: Discover vibrant coral reefs, wrecks, and underwater passageways teeming with marine life.
- Beachcombing: Relax on the island's remote beaches, collect seashells, and take in panoramic views of the Caribbean Sea.

- Waterfront Dining: Enjoy fresh seafood, tropical cocktails, and waterfront dining experiences at seaside restaurants and bars.
- Sunset Cruises: Take a sunset cruise around Isla Carenero and enjoy breathtaking views of the sunset over the horizon.

5.3 Recommended Itineraries for Island Hopping

Here are two recommended paths for island-hopping in Bocas del Toro:

1. Day Trip to the Isla Bastimentos:
- Morning: Depart from Bocas Town for Isla Bastimentos. Explore Red Frog Beach, swim in the azure oceans, and go through the forest pathways.
- Afternoon: Have lunch at a beachside restaurant before going snorkeling or diving at Bastimentos National Marine Park.
- Evening: Return to Bocas Town in the late afternoon and unwind with a meal and beverages at one of the waterfront taverns or eateries.

2. Full-day excursion to Isla Zapatilla:

- Morning: Take a full-day boat cruise to Isla Zapatilla. Snorkel in the clear waters, relax on remote beaches, and explore the island's lush woods.

- Afternoon: Have a picnic lunch on the beach and take a guided nature walk of the island's interior.

- Evening: Return to Bocas Town and dine at a local restaurant before enjoying drinks and live music at a beach bar.

These recommended itineraries provide an idea of the many activities and natural riches that await travelers in Bocas del Toro. Whether you're looking for adventure, relaxation, or cultural immersion, island hopping in Bocas del Toro will provide you with one-of-a-kind experiences and breathtaking discoveries.

Chapter 6

Outdoor Adventures

6.1 Snorkelling and Diving Spots

Bocas del Toro is known for its stunning underwater scenery, vibrant coral reefs, and diverse marine life, making it a snorkeling and diving hotspot. Here are some great snorkeling and diving spots to visit in Bocas del Toro:

1. Coral Garden:
- Coral Gardens, located near Isla Bastimentos, is a popular snorkeling and diving destination known for its vivid coral reefs teeming with marine life such as tropical fish, sea turtles, and eagle rays.
- Dive into the crystal-clear waters to see the amazing coral formations, underwater tunnels, and dazzling sea fans that dot the seabed, creating an enthralling underwater spectacle.

2. Hospital Point:
- Hospital Point, located off the coast of Isla Solarte, is a popular diving location known for

its abundance of marine life and stunning coral formations.

- Explore the depths and uncover a diverse range of marine animals, including reef sharks, stingrays, moray eels, and schools of colorful reef fish.

3. Dolphin Bay:

- Dolphin Bay, located on the leeward side of Isla Cristóbal, is a natural habitat for pods of playful bottlenose dolphins, making it an excellent location for snorkelers and divers to see these incredible creatures in their natural environment.

- Join a guided snorkeling tour and cruise through the tranquil waters of Dolphin Bay, where you may see dolphins frolicking, feeding, and playing in the warm Caribbean sea.

4. Starfish Beach:

- Starfish Beach, located on Isla Colón's western shore, is named for the abundance of colorful starfish that live in the shallow waters around the beach.

- Take your snorkel gear and explore the sandy bottom, where you may come across a kaleidoscope of starfish of different shapes, sizes, and colors, creating a spectacular underwater landscape.

5. The garden:
- The Garden, located off the coast of Isla Carenero, is a popular diving site known for its vibrant coral gardens, towering coral pinnacles, and rich wildlife.
- Explore the depths and uncover a labyrinth of coral formations, swim-throughs, and underwater tunnels inhabited by a diverse range of marine critters such as reef sharks, barracudas, and colorful reef fish.

6. Crawl Cay:
- Located near Isla Bastimentos, Crawl Cay is a hidden gem known for its crystal-clear waters, shallow coral reefs, and diverse marine life.
- Snorkel among the pristine coral reefs to observe a rainbow of colorful fish, playful sea turtles, and curious stingrays that inhabit the diverse underwater ecosystem.

These snorkeling and diving destinations provide a glimpse into the breathtaking beauty and diversity of Bocas del Toro's underwater ecosystem. Whether you're a first-time snorkeler or a seasoned diver, exploring these underwater environments ensures incredible encounters and awe-inspiring moments of wonder beneath the waves.

6.2 Surfing Destinations and Tips.

Bocas del Toro features world-class surfing beaches with consistent waves and breathtaking natural scenery. Here are some significant surfing spots and recommendations for surfers visiting the region:

1. Playa Bluff:
- Playa Bluff is one of the most well-known surfing beaches in Bocas del Toro, with long stretches of sandy beachfront and strong waves that attract surfers from all over the world.
- Experienced surfers may challenge themselves on Playa Bluff's massive reef breaks and fast, hollow waves, while beginners can learn and practice on smaller waves closer to shore.

2. Paunch Beach:

- Paunch Beach is another popular surfing area known for its consistent waves and relaxed atmosphere. The beach offers a variety of waves suitable for surfers of all skill levels, from gentle rollers to strong reef breaks.

- Surf schools and rental companies are available near Paunch Beach, offering training, equipment rentals, and guided surf tours to surfers looking to improve their skills or find new breaks.

3. Wizard Beach:

- Wizard Beach is a secret surfing spot on Isla Bastimentos that may be reached by a scenic stroll through the woods. The beach offers large waves and undisturbed breaks, making it a favorite among experienced surfers looking for adventure and solitude.

Surfing tips:

- Know Your Ability Level: Select surfing places that match your ability level and experience. Beginners should stick to beginner-friendly breakers with tiny waves and sandy bottoms, whilst experienced surfers may try more difficult reef and point breaks.

- Respect Local Regulations and Etiquette: Learn about local surfing rules and etiquette, such as right of way, lineup etiquette, and surfer priority. Respect the local surf community and follow any rules or limits in place to ensure a safe and enjoyable surfing experience for everybody.

- Stay Safe: Pay attention to water conditions, weather forecasts, and potential hazards like rocks, reefs, and strong currents. To reduce the risk of accidents or injuries, always surf within your limits, wear proper safety equipment, and stay aware of your surroundings.

6.3 Hiking Trails and Natural Reserves

Bocas del Toro is home to lush forests, breathtaking waterfalls, and diverse ecosystems waiting to be discovered. Here are several hiking pathways and natural spots to explore in the region:

1. Bastimentos National Marine Park:
- Bastimentos National Marine Park protects a wide area of both marine and terrestrial habitats, including virgin rainforests, mangrove forests, and coral reefs.
- Explore hiking paths that wind through the park's dense forest, giving you the chance to view sloths, monkeys, and exotic birds.

2. Finca Los Monos Botanical Garden:
- Finca Los Monos Botanical Garden is a lush oasis on Isla Bastimentos, with a diverse collection of tropical plants, flowers, and exotic fruits.
- Wander through the garden's meandering walks to discover rare orchids, towering palms, and vibrant butterflies amid the peaceful natural surroundings.

3. Sendero Loma Bastimentos:
- Sendero Loma Bastimentos is a magnificent hiking trail that leads to the highest point of Isla Bastimentos, providing panoramic views of the surrounding islands and coastline.

- Take a guided tour through the forest to the summit of Loma Bastimentos, where you can take in the breathtaking views and learn about the island's diverse wildlife.

4. La Gruta Cave:
- La Gruta Cave is a natural limestone cave on Isla Bastimentos that may be reached after a short hike through the forest.
- Explore the cave's mystical chambers and underground tunnels, which are adorned with stalactites, stalagmites, and ancient rock formations, providing an intriguing glimpse into the region's geological history.

Bocas del Toro offers an abundance of outdoor adventure and exploration opportunities, from lush forest pathways to pristine marine reserves, all set against the stunning backdrop of Panama's Caribbean coast. Whether you're hiking through the rainforest, surfing world-class waves, or snorkeling in crystal-clear waters, the natural wonders of Bocas del Toro await travelers looking for remarkable experiences in paradise.

Chapter 7

Wildlife and Nature

7.1 Wildlife Viewing Opportunities

Bocas del Toro is brimming with biodiversity, providing several possibilities for wildlife enthusiasts to see and interact with the region's distinctive flora and fauna. Here are some of the best wildlife viewing opportunities in Bocas del Toro:

1. Sloths:
- Bocas del Toro is home to two types of sloths: three-toed and two-toed sloths. These unusual species may often be observed hanging from tree branches in the region's lush rainforests, particularly in Bastimentos National Marine Park and Isla Bastimentos.

2. Howler Monkeys:
- The rainforests of Bocas del Toro are home to thousands of howler monkeys, who are known for their distinctive guttural noises that echo through the treetops. Visitors to Isla

Bastimentos and other remote locations may have the opportunity to see these fascinating monkeys in their natural habitat.

3. Red-eyed Tree Frogs:
- The red-eyed tree frog, with its vibrant colors and striking look, represents Central America's tropical rainforests. These unusual amphibians may be found throughout Bocas del Toro, particularly in the lush vegetation surrounding rivers, streams, and ponds.

4. Toucans and parrots:
- Bocas del Toro is a birdwatching refuge where visitors may see a variety of colorful avian species such as toucans, parrots, and hummingbirds. Keep a look out for these feathery beauties in the region's rainforest canopy and along the mangrove forest coasts.

5. Marine life:
- Beneath the surface of the crystal-clear oceans in Bocas del Toro lies a rich underwater habitat brimming with marine life. Snorkelers and divers may see a diverse range of animals,

including tropical fish, reef sharks, sea turtles, and beautiful coral reefs.

6. Dolphins:
- Bottlenose dolphins are commonly sighted in the waters near Bocas del Toro, particularly in Dolphin Bay and other coastal locations. Join a guided dolphin-watching expedition to witness these smart aquatic animals as they swim, play, and frolic in their natural surroundings.

7. Mangrove forests:
- The mangrove forests of Bocas del Toro offer critical habitat for a wide range of animal species, including birds, reptiles, and crabs. Explore the twisting canals and secret channels of the region's mangrove forests to learn about the diverse species that live there.

8. Coral reefs:
- The coral reefs of Bocas del Toro are home to an amazing variety of marine life, such as colorful fish, octopuses, rays, and reef sharks. Snorkelers and divers can explore these active

underwater habitats to see the beauty and diversity of the region's marine wildlife.

Tips for Wildlife Viewing:
- Respect wildlife and the environment: Keep a safe distance from wildlife and avoid disturbing or approaching them in their natural habitat.
- Bring binoculars and cameras to enhance your wildlife-watching experience and capture memorable moments without disturbing the animals.
- Hire Local Guides: Consider hiring a local guide or going on organized wildlife excursions to learn about the region's ecology, behavior, and conservation efforts while admiring its natural beauty.
- Follow Leave No Trace principles to reduce your environmental impact by properly disposing of garbage, staying on authorized paths, and respecting protected areas and animal habitats.

Tourists who visit Bocas del Toro's diverse ecosystems and natural habitats can gain a better understanding of the region's unique biodiversity while also immersing themselves in the wonder and beauty of Panama's Caribbean coast.

7.2 Marine Life and Coral Reef

Bocas del Toro is a snorkeler and diver's dream, thanks to its abundant marine life and spectacular coral reefs. Here's an overview of the marine habitats and coral reefs of Bocas del Toro:

1. Coral reefs:
- Bocas del Toro is home to some of the Caribbean's healthiest coral reefs, distinguished by their vibrant colors, fascinating structures, and diverse marine life.
- Discover coral gardens, reef walls, and underwater pinnacles teeming with tropical fish, crabs, and other aquatic life.

2. Tropical fish:
- The coral reefs of Bocas del Toro provide habitat for a diverse range of tropical fish species, including angelfish, butterflyfish, parrotfish, and sergeant majors.

- Snorkelers and divers may encounter schools of colorful fish darting among the corals, creating a mesmerizing underwater display of movement and color.

3. Sea turtles:
- Bocas del Toro is a popular nesting location for sea turtles such as green turtles, hawksbill turtles, and loggerhead turtles.
- Witness the enchantment of sea turtle nesting season, which typically occurs between March and September, when female turtles flock to the beaches of Bocas del Toro to lay their eggs on the sand.
4. Rays and Sharks:
- Watch beautiful rays and secretive reef sharks glide effortlessly through the crystal-clear waters of Bocas del Toro.
- Dive sites like Hospital Point and Coral Gardens allow you to see these beautiful animals in their natural habitat, against a backdrop of colorful coral formations and underwater scenery.

5. Octopus and eels:

- Explore the depths of Bocas del Toro's coral reefs to discover hidden treasures like octopuses, moray eels, and other rare aquatic species.

- Keep an eye out for camouflaged octopuses that blend seamlessly into their surroundings, as well as secretive eels that emerge from coral cracks in search of food.

Conservation efforts:

- The Coral Repair Foundation and local marine conservation groups are actively involved in coral reef repair and preservation initiatives in Bocas del Toro.

- Visitors may contribute to conservation efforts by practicing safe snorkeling and diving, participating in reef monitoring programs, and learning about the importance of preserving marine ecosystems for future generations.

7.3 Birdwatching Hotspots

Bocas del Toro is a birdwatcher's paradise, with a diverse range of avian species and pristine natural habitats to discover. Here are some of the best birding locations in the region:

1. Isla Bastimentos National Marine Park:
- Visit Isla Bastimentos National Marine Park's lush rainforests and mangrove woods to witness a variety of bird species such as toucans, parrots, trogons, and herons.
- Take a guided birdwatching tour or explore the park's network of hiking trails to discover hidden birding gems and see birds in their natural habitat.

2. Red Frog Beach:
- Red Frog Beach and its surrounding rainforest are home to a wide diversity of bird species, including the unusual red-eyed tree frog and a spectrum of colorful songbirds.
- Wander along the wooded walks and listen for the delightful calls of birds booming over the canopy, or scan the treetops for glimpses of elusive species darting among the trees.

3. Isla Solarte:
- Isla Solarte is a lovely island located just a short boat journey from Bocas Town, affording outstanding birding possibilities amid its lush vegetation and coastal mangroves.
- Explore the island's hiking pathways, marshes, and coastal habitats to witness a variety of bird species, including herons, egrets, kingfishers, and woodpeckers.

4. Dolphin Bay:
- Dolphin Bay is not only a hotspot for dolphin-watching but also a popular birding destination, with its tranquil oceans and mangrove-lined shores bringing a variety of coastal and migratory bird species.
- Keep an eye out for ospreys, frigatebirds, pelicans, and herons soaring overhead or lounging along the shore as you sail across the bay on a guided birding adventure.

5. Bird Island (Isla Pájaros):
- Bird Island, also known as Isla Pájaros, is a tiny islet located within the borders of Isla

Bastimentos National Marine Park, home to breeding colonies of seabirds and shorebirds.
- Take a boat journey to Bird Island and see the spectacle of hundreds of birds nesting, feeding, and soaring over the island's steep cliffs and mangrove woodlands.

Whether you're exploring lush rainforests, coastal wetlands, or pristine island habitats, Bocas del Toro gives unlimited options for birdwatchers to engage with nature and witness the various avian species that make this tropical paradise home.

Chapter 8

Cultural Experiences

8.1 Indigenous Communities and Traditions

Bocas del Toro is not only blessed with natural beauty but also a rich cultural past, including indigenous tribes with unique traditions and customs. Here's a look at the Indigenous traditions and practices of Bocas del Toro:

1. Ngöbe-Buglé Indigenous People:
- The Ngöbe-Buglé is one of the primary indigenous populations of Panama, having a substantial presence in the Bocas del Toro region. They have a rich cultural past, distinguished by traditional traditions, language, and handicrafts.
- Visitors get the option to learn about Ngöbe-Buglé culture via community-based tourism programs that provide insights into their way of life, including traditional farming practices, artisanal crafts, and spiritual beliefs.

2. Emberá Indigenous People:
- The Emberá are another indigenous group having a presence in Bocas del Toro, notably in the secluded rainforest areas of the region. They are famous for their bright traditional attire, sophisticated handicrafts, and dramatic song and dance performances.
- Travelers may engage in cultural exchanges with Emberá tribes, partaking in traditional ceremonies, learning about medicinal plants, and experiencing the art of Emberá basket weaving and wood carving.

3. Traditional Medicine and Healing Practices:
- Indigenous inhabitants in Bocas del Toro have a great connection to the natural environment and rely on traditional medicine and healing skills passed down through generations.
- Visitors may learn about the medicinal properties of native plants and herbs utilized in traditional healing practices, as well as participate in lectures and demonstrations led by local healers and shamans.

4. Artisanal crafts and textiles:

- Ngöbe-Buglé and Emberá artisans are famous for their exceptional goods, including woven baskets, exquisite textiles, and beautiful beading.
- Travelers may purchase unique things directly from local artisans or attend artisan fairs and cooperatives that promote indigenous cultures and foster sustainable living.

5. Cultural Festivals and Celebrations:
- Throughout the year, Bocas del Toro organizes a number of cultural events and celebrations that reflect the region's distinct indigenous customs.
- From traditional dances and music performances to gourmet festivals and spiritual ceremonies, these activities allow tourists a unique opportunity to immerse themselves in indigenous culture and traditions.

6. Environmental stewardship:
- Indigenous peoples of Bocas del Toro play an important role in environmental stewardship and conservation efforts, serving as guardians

of the region's natural resources and ecosystems.

- Visitors may engage in eco-tourism activities that benefit indigenous conservation initiatives, including community-managed ecotourism programs and sustainable agriculture practices.

Discovering the cultural history of indigenous settlements in Bocas del Toro allows travelers to have a better understanding of Panama's diverse cultural tapestry and form meaningful connections with the people who live here. Visitors who engage in ethical and polite tourism activities may help to preserve and appreciate indigenous cultures for many years to come.

8.2 Local Festivals and Events

Bocas del Toro is a booming hub of cultural festivals and events, giving visitors a unique opportunity to immerse themselves in the region's rich history and vibrant culture. Here are some local festivals and events to explore in Bocas del Toro:

1. Bocas del Toro Carneval:
- The Bocas del Toro Carnaval is an annual celebration that takes place in February or March and features colorful parades, music, dancing, and street performances.
- Join locals and visitors alike as they dress up in colorful costumes and masks, dance to traditional music, and participate in lively festivities showcasing Panama's rich culture on the Caribbean coast.

2. Bocas Del Toro Reggae Festival:
- The Bocas del Toro Reggae Festival is an annual music festival held in August that celebrates the region's love of reggae music and Caribbean culture.
- Enjoy live music performances by local and international reggae performers, dance to the infectious sounds of reggae, ska, and dancehall music, and soak up the laid-back atmosphere of this iconic Caribbean festival.

3. International Chocolate Festival:
- The International Chocolate event is a scrumptious chocolate event that takes place in

Bocas del Toro every year, usually in September or October.
- Participate in chocolate tastings, lectures, and culinary demonstrations that showcase the many flavors and variants of Panamanian cacao, as well as learn about the chocolate-making process from bean to bar.

4. Dia de la Etnia Negra (Day of Black Ethnicity)
- Dia de la Etnia Negra is an annual cultural festival held on May 30th to honor the achievements and heritage of Afro-Panamanian communities in Bocas del Toro and beyond.
- Enjoy traditional Afro-Caribbean music and dance performances, cultural exhibits, and culinary delights that celebrate the resilience, originality, and cultural identity of Panama's Afro-descendant population.

5. Semana Santa (holy week):
- Semana Santa, or Holy Week, is a religious celebration celebrated across Panama, including Bocas del Toro, in the week before Easter Sunday.

- Witness religious processions, traditional rituals, and cultural events that highlight this holy time in Panama's Catholic calendar, as locals and visitors come together to reflect, pray, and celebrate.

8.3 Artisan Markets and Craft Workshop

Bocas del Toro is a treasure trove of artisan markets, craft studios, and creative spaces where visitors may purchase locally crafted goods and learn about traditional crafts. Here are several artisan markets and craft studios to visit in Bocas del Toro:

1. Bocas Town Artisan Market:
- The Bocas Town Artisan Market is a bustling marketplace located in the heart of Bocas Town, offering a diverse assortment of handmade crafts, textiles, jewelry, and souvenirs made by local artisans.
- Explore vibrant marketplaces and shops selling traditional Ngöbe-Buglé and Emberá items like woven baskets, beaded jewelry, hand-carved masks, and embroidered linens.

2. La Buga Arts and Crafts Workshop:
- La Buga Art & Craft Workshop is a creative space in Bocas Town where visitors may participate in hands-on craft classes led by local craftspeople.
- Learn how to weave baskets, make pottery, or carve traditional masks, and create your own one-of-a-kind masterpiece to take home as a remembrance of your trip to Bocas del Toro.

3. The Bocatoreño Market
El Mercadito Bocatoreño is a small artisan market in Bocas Town that sells handmade products, artwork, and souvenirs created by local artists and artisans.
- Shop for one-of-a-kind gifts and souvenirs while supporting local craftspeople and discovering unique treasures like hand-painted ceramics, upcycled glassware, and indigenous-inspired textiles.

4. Artisan Workshops and Studios:
- Explore Bocas Town's passageways to discover hidden artisan workshops and studios where local artists and craftsmen create their work.

- Visit pottery studios, jewelry workshops, and painting ateliers to see the creative process firsthand as artisans transform raw materials into works of art inspired by the beauty and culture of Bocas del Toro.

5. Cultural experiences and workshops:
- Attend cultural events and workshops hosted by local organizations and community groups, where you may learn traditional crafts, culinary techniques, and creative activities from indigenous and Afro-Panamanian artisans.
- Participate in meaningful cultural exchanges and connect with locals while learning about Bocas del Toro's rich cultural history and artistic practices.

Visitors to Bocas del Toro may immerse themselves in Panama's vibrant arts and crafts scene by attending artisan markets, craft workshops, and cultural events. They can also support local craftspeople while discovering one-of-a-kind products and experiences to treasure for a lifetime.

Chapter 9

Sustainable Travel Tips

9.1 Environmentally Friendly Practices for Visitors

As visitors, we have a responsibility to reduce our impact on the environment and encourage sustainable tourism practices that preserve the natural beauty and cultural legacy of places like Bocas del Toro. Here are some eco-friendly habits that travelers should consider.

1. Reduce, reuse, and recycle:
- Practice responsible waste management by reducing single-use plastics, recycling wherever possible, and properly disposing of rubbish in designated containers.
- Bring a reusable water bottle, shopping bag, and cutlery to reduce plastic waste and promote environmentally friendly alternatives.

2. Conserve water and energy.
- During your visit, save water and energy by taking shorter showers, shutting off lights and

electronics when not in use, and using energy-efficient equipment.

- Encourage accommodations and businesses that promote sustainability and conservation, such as eco-lodges and eco-friendly tour operators.

3. Choose sustainable transportation:

- To reduce carbon emissions, use sustainable modes of transportation such as walking, biking, or public transportation while touring Bocas del Toro.

- Consider carpooling or sharing rides with other passengers to lessen environmental impact and support local transportation providers.

4. Respect wildlife and natural habitats.

- Keep a safe distance from wildlife and avoid feeding, petting, or disturbing them in their natural surroundings.

To prevent ecological impact and sustain biodiversity, stay on permitted trails, respect protected areas and animal habitats, and follow the Leave No Trace principles.

5. Support local conservation efforts:
- Take part in environmentally responsible excursions and activities that support conservation initiatives, such as wildlife monitoring programs, beach clean-ups, and coral reef restoration projects.
- Contribute to local conservation organizations and community-based projects in Bocas del Toro that encourage environmental stewardship and sustainable development.

6. Learn about the local culture and traditions.
- Learn about the cultural heritage and traditions of Bocas del Toro's indigenous and Afro-Panamanian communities, and respect their practices, beliefs, and way of life.
- Support local artists, crafters, and cultural initiatives by purchasing handmade things, attending cultural events, and engaging in meaningful cultural exchanges.

7. Leave just footprints:
- Leave natural and cultural areas in the same condition you found them, taking care not to

litter, deface, or remove artifacts or natural specimens.

- Bring images and memories back with you, leaving only footprints and a positive impact on the people and places you visit.

Visitors to Bocas del Toro can help to protect its natural and cultural heritage by adopting eco-friendly habits and supporting sustainable tourism initiatives, as well as creating important and memorable experiences for both tourists and locals. Together, we can help to preserve the beauty and diversity of Bocas del Toro for future generations to enjoy.

9.2 Responsible Tourism Initiatives

Responsible tourism initiatives play an important role in promoting sustainable development and preserving the natural and cultural heritage of places like Bocas del Toro. Here are a few ethical tourism initiatives to support:

1. Community-Based Tourism Programs:
- Take part in community-based tourism projects that enable local communities to benefit directly from tourism while preserving their cultural traditions and natural resources.
- Stay in locally owned motels, eat at family-run restaurants, and support small businesses that reinvest in the community and create significant job opportunities.

2. Sustainable Tour Operators:
- Select tour operators and travel groups that prioritize sustainability, environmental stewardship, and responsible tourism practices.
- Look for eco-certifications, cooperation with local communities, and initiatives that decrease environmental impact while providing positive social and economic benefits to host communities.

3. Wildlife Conservation Projects:
- Support wildlife conservation projects and initiatives that protect endangered species, preserve natural habitats, and promote responsible wildlife tourism.

- Volunteer with reputable conservation organizations, participate in wildlife monitoring programs and help to research and conservation efforts to preserve biodiversity in Bocas del Toro.

4. Cultural Preservation Programs:
- Participate in cultural preservation programs and events that honor and preserve the traditional heritage of Bocas del Toro's indigenous and Afro-Panamanian communities.
- Participate in cultural events, seminars, and festivals that celebrate traditional music, dance, crafts, and culinary traditions, as well as support local artisans and cultural programs that promote cultural diversity and interchange.

5. Environmental Education and Awareness:
- Support environmental education and awareness activities that promote sustainable lifestyles, conservation practices, and responsible tourism behavior among tourists and local communities.

- Take part in eco-tours, guided nature walks, and educational programs that educate visitors about the value of biodiversity, ecosystem conservation, and environmental stewardship in Bocas del Toro.

9.3 Supporting Local Conservation Efforts.

Local conservation efforts are critical to preserving the natural habitats, biodiversity, and cultural legacy of Bocas del Toro. Here is how you may support local conservation efforts:

1. Donate to conservation organizations.
- Provide financial support to local conservation groups, non-profits, and grassroots projects dedicated to environmental protection and sustainable development in Bocas del Toro.
- Consider making donations or participating in fundraising campaigns to benefit conservation projects, habitat restoration efforts, and community-based conservation programs.

2. Volunteer for conservation projects.

- Contribute your time and expertise to conservation projects and initiatives in Bocas del Toro, such as wildlife monitoring, habitat restoration, beach cleanups, and environmental education programs.

- Join volunteer organizations, conservation groups, and community-based initiatives that rely on volunteer assistance to carry out conservation activities and achieve conservation goals.

3. Participate in citizen science programs.

- Participate in citizen science activities and research programs that collect data on biodiversity, environmental health, and ecosystem dynamics in Bocas del Toro.

- Help scientific research and monitoring programs by reporting animal sightings, collecting field data, and taking part in research trips and monitoring surveys conducted by conservation organizations and academic institutions.

4. Advocate for conservation policies.

- Advocate for laws and regulations that promote environmental preservation, sustainable development, and responsible tourism in Bocas del Toro and beyond.

- Support initiatives that maintain natural habitats, wildlife corridors, and marine ecosystems, as well as advocate for the passage of legislation and regulations that protect the environment and ensure the long-term preservation of Bocas del Toro's natural and cultural heritage.

Tourists who support responsible tourism programs and local conservation efforts may help to preserve Bocas del Toro's beauty, biodiversity, and cultural richness for future years. Together, we can have a positive impact and contribute to the long-term development and conservation of this unique and valuable place.

Chapter 10

Safety and Practical Information

10.1 Health and Safety Advice for Travelers

Ensuring your health and safety is vital while visiting Bocas del Toro. Here are some crucial health and safety concerns for travelers:

1. Stay hydrated:
- Drink plenty of water, especially in the tropical atmosphere of Bocas del Toro, to keep hydrated and prevent dehydration and heat-related disorders.

2. Use Sun Protection:
- Apply sunscreen with a high SPF rating, wear sunglasses, and wear protective garments to protect yourself from the sun's harmful UV rays, especially during outdoor activities.

3. Prevent Mosquito Bites:
- Protect yourself against mosquito-borne illnesses by using insect repellent containing

DEET, wearing long sleeves and pants during dawn and twilight when mosquitoes are most active, and sleeping beneath mosquito nets if needed.

4. Stay Updated on Vaccinations:
- Consult with your healthcare practitioner before coming to Bocas del Toro to ensure that your immunizations are up-to-date, including routine vaccinations and travel-specific vaccines like hepatitis A and typhoid.

5. Practice Food and Water Safety:
- Stick to bottled or filtered water, and avoid consuming tap water or ice cubes in drinks to prevent waterborne diseases.
- Eat freshly prepared and well-cooked meals from reputable restaurants, and avoid consuming raw or undercooked seafood and street food to decrease the risk of foodborne diseases.

6. Be mindful of ocean safety.
- Exercise caution when swimming, snorkeling, or indulging in aquatic activities, and heed

warnings about strong currents, rip tides, and deadly marine organisms such as jellyfish and sea urchins.

- Only swim in designated swimming areas with lifeguards present; avoid swimming alone or in remote areas without supervision.

7. Secure your belongings:

- Keep your valuables, including passports, money, and electronics, secure and out of sight to deter theft and reduce the risk of pickpocketing and minor crimes.

- Keep important documents and goods in hotel safes or locked lockboxes when visiting Bocas del Toro.

8. Stay informed:

- Stay informed about local safety and security circumstances in Bocas del Toro by monitoring news updates, following travel advisories issued by your government, and seeking information from local authorities and hotel workers as needed.

- Be aware of your surroundings and trust your instincts if you feel uncomfortable or unsafe in any situation.

9. Carry emergency contacts.

- Keep a list of emergency contacts, such as local emergency services, your country's embassy or consulate, and your travel insurance provider's contact information, in case of an emergency or unanticipated event.

10. Purchase travel insurance.

- Consider purchasing comprehensive travel insurance to cover medical emergencies, trip cancellations, and travel delays during your time in Bocas del Toro.

By following these health and safety rules and using caution and common sense, you may have a safe and enjoyable vacation to Bocas del Toro, Panama. Remember to prioritize your well-being and take the necessary precautions to guarantee a comfortable and enjoyable travel.

10.2 Money & Currency Exchange

When traveling to Bocas del Toro, it is essential to be aware of money difficulties and currency conversion options. Here's what you should know:

1. Currency:
- Panama's official currency is the Balboa (PAB), which is tied to the US dollar (USD). However, in truth, the USD is actively used and acknowledged throughout Panama, including Bocas del Toro.

2. Currency Exchange:
- Although the Balboa is the official currency, US dollars are the most often used for transactions in Bocas del Toro. It is better to carry small USD denominations for convenience, since larger notes may be more difficult to break, especially in tiny locales.
- Currency exchange services are available in banks, exchange offices, and some hotels in Bocas del Toro. Be careful of exchange rates and currency conversion fees, and check pricing to get the most value for your money.

3. ATMs and Credit cards:

- ATMs are widely available in Bocas del Toro, particularly in Bocas Town and adjacent urban regions. Most ATMs accept major international debit and credit cards, such as Visa and MasterCard. However, you must notify your bank of your holiday plans in order to avoid any issues with card usage abroad.

- Credit cards are widely accepted at hotels, restaurants, and other significant institutions in Bocas del Toro. However, smaller businesses and street vendors may prefer cash transactions, so it's always a good idea to have some cash on hand for small purchases and transactions.

4. Traveler's checks:

- While traveler's checks were formerly a popular method of secure money conversion, they are now less often used due to the widespread acceptance of credit cards and the availability of ATMs. It may be difficult to find restaurants in Bocas del Toro that accept traveler's cheques, therefore it is recommended that you use another method of payment.

5. Exchange Rates and Fees:

- Be aware of exchange rates and fees associated with currency conversion, ATM withdrawals, and credit card transactions. Banks and exchange offices may charge commission fees or provide less favorable conversion rates, so it is critical to compare rates and expenses before making a currency transaction.

10.3 Emergency Contacts and Relevant Resources

It is essential to have access to relevant contact information and resources throughout your stay in Bocas del Toro, whether in the event of an emergency or to access useful services. Here are some key links and resources:

1. Emergency services:
- Emergency Police: Call 911.
- Fire Department: Call 911.
- Medical Emergencies: Call 911.

2. Hospitals and medical centers:
- Hospital Bolívar: +507 757-9086.
- Hospital Regional de Bocas del Toro, +507 757-9237

3. Tourist Information Centers:
- Bocas del Toro Tourism Office: +507 757-9558.
- Bocas del Toro Tourist Police: +507 757-9143.

4. Embassy and Consulate Information:
- Embassy of the United States in Panama City: +507 317-5000.
- Embassy of Canada in Panama City: +507 294-2500.
- Embassy of the United Kingdom in Panama Ama City: +507 297-6400.

5. Useful resources:
- The tourism website for Bocas del Toro is [www.visitbocasdeltoro.com].
- The Panama Tourism Authority's website is [www.visitpanama.com].
- Bocas del Toro weather forecast: www.weather.com.

6. Travel insurance providers:

- Contact your travel insurance provider for assistance with medical emergencies, trip disruptions, and other travel-related issues during your stay in Bocas del Toro.

Having access to emergency contacts and essential information may provide peace of mind and help you deal with any unexpected situations or problems that may arise during your trip to Bocas Del Toro. Keep these contacts handy and stay informed about local services and help available to travelers in the area.

Made in the USA
Las Vegas, NV
21 September 2024

95571177R00056